Respiration and Photosynthesis

Revised Edtion

Donna Latham

capstone

a division of Capstone Global Library, LLC.
Chicago, Illinois

To contact Capstone Global Library, please
call 800-747-4992, or visit our web site
www.mycapstone.com

Editorial: Megan Cotugno and Andrew Farrow
Design: Philippa Jenkins
Illustrations: KJA-artists.com
Picture Research: Ruth Blair
Production: Alison Parsons
Originated by Modern Age

Library of Congress Cataloging-in-Publication Data
Library of Congress Cataloging-in-Publication Data is available on the Library of Congress website.

ISBN: 978-1-4109-8632-0 (paperback)
ISBN: 978-1-4109-8648-1 (ebook pdf)

Acknowledgments
Alamy: Chronicle, 28, 31, Joe Federer, 13; Capstone Press, 22-23, 39; Dreamstime: Vlue, 33; Getty Images: Ron Boardman, 12; iStockphoto: Kwanchai6632, top 25, yoh4nn, 42; NASA: SDO, 6; Newscom: A3250 Oliver Berg Deutsch Presse Agentur, top 41, Album /Prisma, 30-31; Science Source: David M. Phillips/Mary Martin, 37, P. Dayanandan, 14; Shutterstock: Aleksey Stemmer, 21, Ami Parikh, 32, Andrei Medvedev, 43, ANYPIC, 5, Aptyp_koK, Cover, 1, 8-9, bamenic181, top 7, Bildagentur Zoonar GmbH, 24, cobraphotography, 16, davemhuntphotography, bottom 41, Fotofermer, 17, lamTK, 40, Jordan Tan, Cover, 26, mahey, 20, Matt Tilghman, 4, oticki, bottom 25, Pat_Hastings, bottom 7, Patty Chan, 10, Peter Zijlstra, 15, photoiconix, 11, photoinnovation, 38, Pierre Leclerc, 34, s_oleg, 35, Samantzis, bottom 19, Stuart G Porter, 1, 19, Yellowj, design element throughout

The publishers would like to thank literacy consultants Nancy Harris, Patti Suerth, and Monica Szalaj, and content consultant Dr. Ted Dolter for their assistance in the preparation of this book.

Some words are shown in bold, **like this**. These words are explained in the glossary. You will find important information and definitions underlined and in bold, **like this**.

Printed and bound in the United States of America.
072419 002467

Contents

What is this consumer, and how fast can it run?

Go to page 19!

What amazing process occurs in chloroplasts?

Find out on page 9

Breathing Buddies

Plants are critical for life. They produce oxygen necessary for our survival. Unlike other living things, plants make their own food. This process is photosynthesis. Through respiration, plants break down food and release carbon dioxide and water.

Plants are your breathing buddies. They are your prized partners in obtaining oxygen. Oxygen, a colorless, odorless gas, keeps you alive. Unlike other living things, plants have an amazing ability. They make their own food. This process is called photosynthesis.

Through the process of respiration, plants use oxygen to break down sugar and get energy from food they make. As a result, plants give off water and carbon dioxide.

The terms are the same. Yet, the processes of plant respiration and human respiration are different. The function of the human respiratory system is to exchange gases. It takes in oxygen and releases carbon dioxide. In people, oxygen reaches **cells** and tissues through the blood.

Rainforests like this produce a great deal of oxygen on our planet.

Take a Deep Breath...And Thank a Plant!

Did you know that every cell in your body needs oxygen? Without it, cells would die off. And so would you! When you breathe, you inhale oxygen. You exhale carbon dioxide. That's another colorless, odorless gas. Take a deep breath through your nose. As you do, oxygen enters your body. Now, exhale from your mouth. You've just puffed carbon dioxide into the air. Through photosynthesis, plants consume that carbon dioxide. They release oxygen—so you can enjoy another breath.

Please Pass the Sun

Some scientists believe photosynthesis is the planet's most important process. Without it, people and animals would have no food. Earth would lack building materials for homes and businesses.

Living things thrive on the Sun's energy. Through photosynthesis, plants capture energy from the Sun and convert it in a chemical reaction. Through the food chain, they pass it along. Discover why photosynthesis is key to survival.

Many scientists think photosynthesis is the key to the survival of most of the food chain.

Photosynthesis Begins with the Sun

The Sun is the source of energy on Earth. Called solar energy, it heats Earth. It controls weather and plays a role in photosynthesis.

Solar Energy

Solar energy radiates over our planet in the form of light. It is easy to see its visible light when the sky is bright with sunshine and you can feel its warmth.

Is it gloomy with clouds today? This doesn't matter! No matter what the conditions are, solar energy heats Earth. It keeps us warm. It's also the source of power that drives weather.

Sunshine holds incredible power—life power! The Sun provides energy for nearly all of Earth's living things. **The sun's energy is called solar energy.**

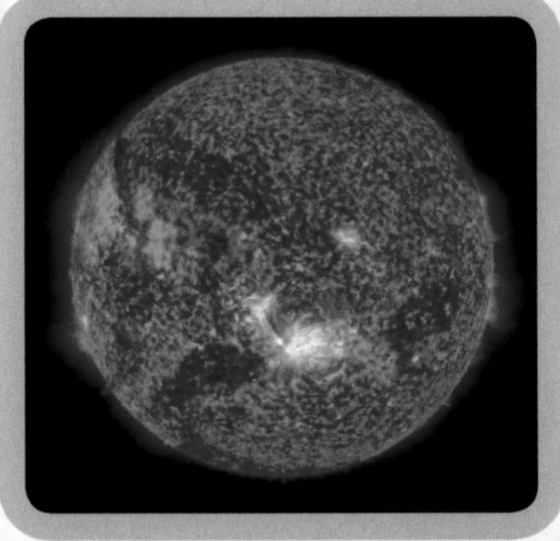

This NASA image captured a solar flare, a short, sudden burst of energy from the sun.

Life Processes

Biologists identify seven life processes common to all living things. To carry out these processes, organisms must have energy.

Movement—being able to move

Respiration—receiving energy from food

Sensitivity—responding to stimuli or changes

Growth—becoming larger

Reproduction—making more of itself

Excretion—passing out wastes

Nutrition—taking in food

Need a shortcut to remember an organism's life processes? **MRS. GREN** is glad to help.

Leaves

Photosynthesis takes place in leaves. Leaves are typically broad and flat. Their wide, thin surfaces allow them to capture as much sunlight as possible. Leaves even grow toward sunlight to catch more rays! Observe phototropism in action to see for yourself.

These leaves will grow toward the sun to capture its light.

What is solar energy?
It's energy from the sun.

Through photosynthesis, plants turn sunlight into what?
It becomes chemical energy.

How do other living things receive the sun's energy?
Plants pass it along through the food chain.

Activity

Phototropism: Growing to the Light

Phototropism is specifically growing toward light.

- Place a plant on a sunny ledge.
- Notice, over time, how the plant curves and grows toward the light source.
- How many days does it take for the plant to bend? What happens to the leaves?
- What happens if you turn the pot so the plant faces away from the light?

Phototropism at work

Understanding Photosynthesis

The word photosynthesis means "to put something together with light." Plants use sunlight, water, and carbon dioxide in photosynthesis. Leaves contain special parts that are specialized for photosynthesis.

Getting to the "Root" of the Word

The word *photosynthesis* is made up of two parts, *photo* and *synthesis*. Photo means "light." When you observed *phototropism*, you watched a plant grow toward light. *Synthesis* means "to put something together." So *photosynthesis* means "to put something together with light." The process of photosynthesis has two stages. One requires sunlight, and the other does not.

Leaves: Food Factories

Leaves are a plant's food factories. Leaves are made of specialized **cells.** They have specific jobs to tackle. **Mesophyll** cells, between layers of leaves, contain **chloroplasts**. Chloroplasts are **organelles**, plant parts with their own jobs. It's in chloroplasts that the amazing process of photosynthesis occurs. Water and carbon dioxide, raw materials of photosynthesis, enter the leaves' cells. Sugar and oxygen, products of photosynthesis, exit.

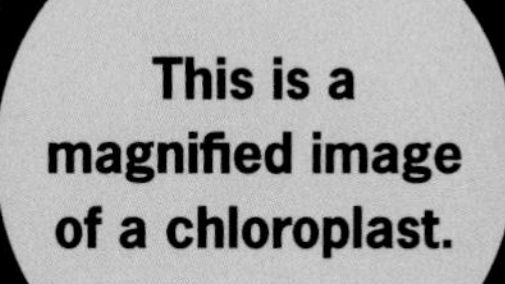

This is a magnified image of a chloroplast.

Inside Leaves

Along with sunlight and carbon dioxide, plants need water to perform photosynthesis. To grow, plants also need nutrients. Where do nutrients come from? Nutrients are in soil. They are transported from roots, up through stems, and then into leaves.

This leaf is a plant organ constructed for photosynthesis.

Leaves are major plant organs. Organs are built from tissues, and tissues are built from **cells**. So how are leaves constructed for photosynthesis? Let's take a closer look at their parts. Study the cross section on the next page to learn more about their special features.

Leaf Cross Section

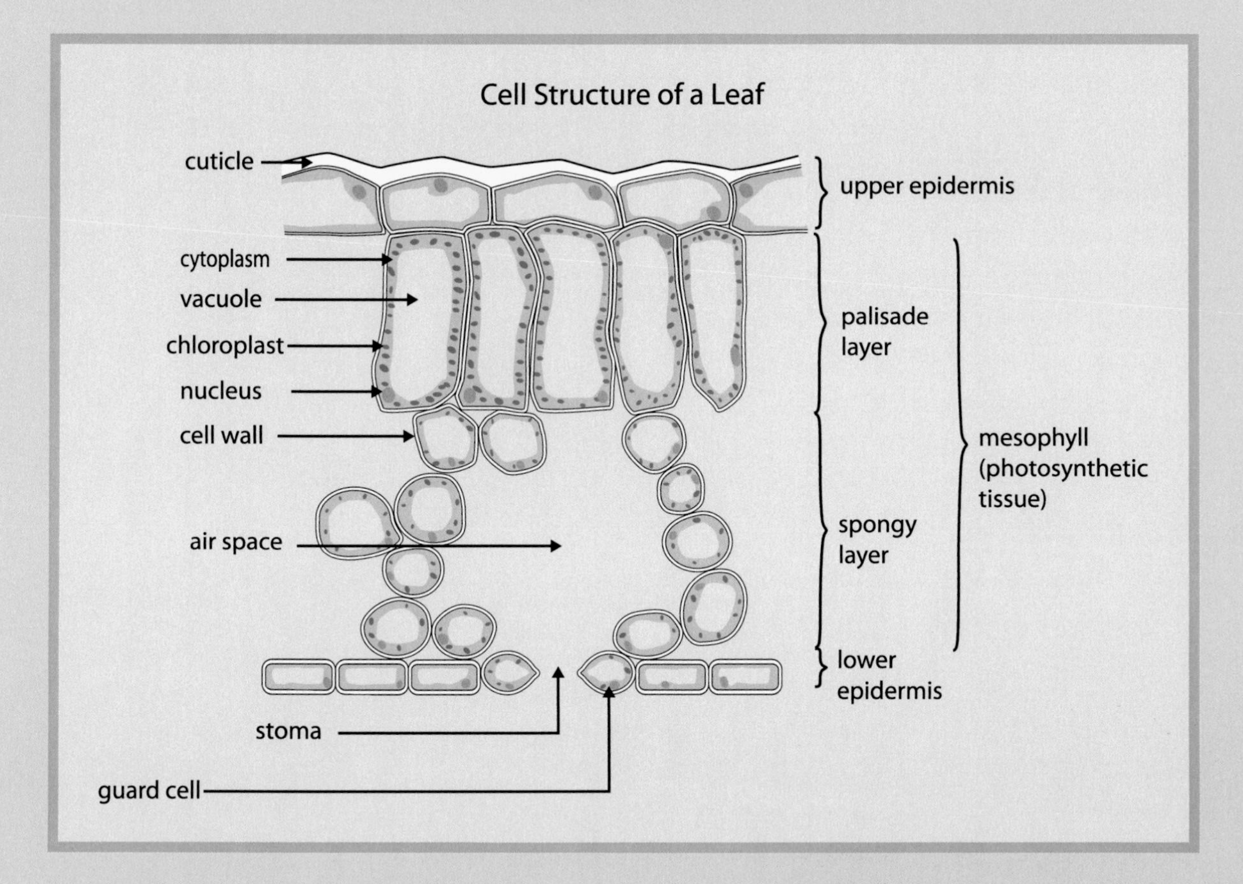

The **cuticle** is a noncellular layer. That means it's not divided into cells. The cuticle seals the leaf from water loss. When you get dehydrated, you might feel sluggish. If too much water evaporates, then the same thing happens to photosynthesis. It slows down.

Just beneath the cuticle is the **epidermis.** The flat cells of the epidermis are rigid. As you know, leaves come in a wide variety of shapes. The protective cells of the epidermis provide shape.

Guard cells are like trap doors in the epidermis. They control **stomata**, which open and shut like mouths. Guard cells allow stomata to take in carbon dioxide and release water and oxygen.

Whipping Up Plant Food

You've learned leaves are food factories. What ingredients does a leaf need to whip up a recipe? In the "light" stage, it requires energy from sunlight. It also needs water (H_2O) from soil and carbon dioxide (CO_2) from air.

Chloroplasts are pint-sized solar panels! Inside them is **chlorophyll**, a green pigment. Chlorophyll gives plants their beautiful shades of green. It snatches solar energy and helps chloroplasts do their job. Plants suck water from the ground through roots. They take in carbon dioxide through stomata.

Stomata (shown here) take in air. They are able to open and close.

Next, in the "dark" stage, chloroplasts get to work on photosynthesis. They turn the three ingredients into **carbohydrates**, such as glucose, a simple sugar. The glucose makes energy for the plant's life processes. These carbohydrates feed the plants—and so much more. Through the food chain (see page 22) they also fuel animals and people. Finally, the stomata release oxygen, which people and animals need to breathe and live. When plants respire, or use energy from food, they use oxygen, too.

<u>**Equation for Photosynthesis**</u>

Plants convert solar energy to chemical energy through photosynthesis. The equation for photosynthesis uses symbols for the process.

$$6CO_2 + 6H_2O + \text{light} \rightarrow C_6H_{12}O_6 + 6O_2$$

Carbon dioxide + water + light → glucose + oxygen

<u>**How does this equation translate? Carbon dioxide, water, and light convert to glucose and oxygen.**</u>

Stomata: Like Lungs and Sweat Glands

Beneath the epidermis are spongy cells. They are plump with chloroplasts. These cells handle the job of making food for the plant. At the bottom of the leaf are stomata. These tiny pores open and close. Similar to lungs, stomata take in air. Like sweat glands in your skin, they allow water to pass. In dry conditions, stomata clamp shut. They make sure plants don't lose too much water.

Veins

In the human body, veins carry blood to the heart. Leaves also contain veins. When you hold a leaf up to the light, you can see them clearly. When you touch them, veins feel stiff. Like miniature pipelines, veins carry water through the leaf. You will learn more about veins, a plant's transportation system, in the next pages.

Activity
Clogged Pores

You'll need a leafy houseplant, such as ivy or pothos, petroleum jelly, and a sunny location.

- Make certain the plant you use is thriving. It should have plenty of leaves.
- Select five large, healthy leaves. GENTLY cover their lower sides with petroleum jelly. Take care not to twist the leaves off the stems.
- Then place the plant on a sunny windowsill.
- Over a one-week period, observe the plant. What's happening to the coated leaves?

What conclusions can you draw about what occurs when stomata become clogged?

This vine is obviously thriving and growing. It has many healthy green leaves.

Plant Tissues

Groups of cells that work together to tackle the same job form tissues. There are three major plant tissue types. They are dermal, ground, and vascular tissues.

Dermal tissues protect soft parts of plants. The epidermis is a dermal tissue. It covers the outside of a plant with a waxy coating.

Ground tissues support stems and roots. They function in photosynthesis and store food in leaves, stems, and roots.

Vascular tissues are transportation systems. They include **xylem** and **phloem** tissues. Xylem carries water and dissolved minerals up from roots. It moves them through the stem and leaves. Phloem moves food made in photosynthesis. It carries sugar through the whole plant, all the way down to the roots. This movement of water, minerals, and sugar is called **translocation.**

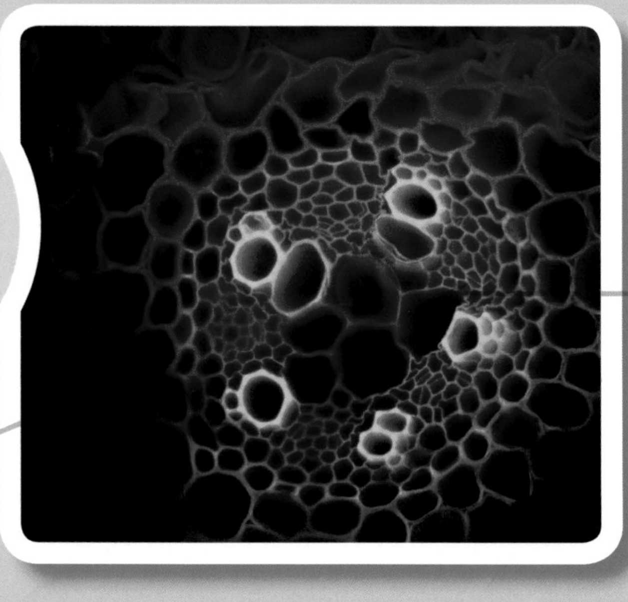

The xylem and phloem are visible in this magnified photo of vascular tissue.

What are stomata?
They are tiny pores that take in air and allow water to pass through leaves.
In which part of the plant does photosynthesis take place?
It's in chloroplasts.
Which tissues serve as a plant transportation system?
Xylem and phloem move water, minerals, and sugar through plants.

Activity

Xylem in Action

You'll need a stalk of celery, a clear jar filled with water, food coloring, and scissors.

1. Make certain the jar is about two-thirds full. Then, add several drops of food coloring. Stir thoroughly.
2. Now, place the celery stalk in the water. Be sure the leaves point up.
3. During a four-hour period, check the stalk every hour. Take notes about any changes.
4. Leave the celery in the water overnight. Check it the following morning. What's happened to the leaves?
5. With adult supervision, CAREFULLY use the scissors to snip away one centimeter at the bottom of the stalk.

You should see tiny colored dots, which are xylem.

What did these pipelines do in the plant?

When you eat celery stalks, you are eating parts of plants.

Tubers, stems, fruits, and nuts

Through photosynthesis, plants make sugars and carbohydrates. Plants use them for food and materials to grow. One carbohydrate that plants make is **starch**. The plant stores starch in stems, fruits, and seed tubers (such as potatoes). Plants use starches to grow and reproduce. They stash some to use during periods where there is little sunlight.

The Sun's energy transfers to people and animals through foods they eat. Carbohydrates, for example, supply high energy. When you enjoy a baked potato or a chunk of lasagna, you are ingesting starch. As starch mixes with oxygen from the air you breathe, you "burn" it off.

Potatoes are a staple in many North American and European diets. They are actually plant tubers. They store carbohydrates during photosynthesis.

Activity

Starch Test

Want to find out if a leaf has photosynthesized? Test it for starch! You'll need two pothos plants, two Petri dishes, 20% iodine solution, forceps, paper towels, two clean microscope slides, and a microscope.

1. Place one plant in a sunny location. Stash the other in a cabinet or covered box where it won't receive light.
2. Check the plants each day for one week. Water them as needed.
3. Then, remove one leaf from each plant. With adult supervision, CAREFULLY cut a 3-millimeter slice from each leaf.
4. Place one strip in each Petri dish with the iodine solution. Then, soak the two leaf strips overnight.
5. Use the forceps to remove each leaf from its Petri dish. Drain the leaves on the paper towels.
6. With the forceps, place the leaf strips on clean slides. Then examine them under the microscope.
7. You should see dark areas of iodine pigment where there are starch granules. How are the two leaf strips different?

Review Activity

Use what you've learned to write a recipe for photosynthesis. Include ingredients and instructions, as you see above.

Vital to a Living Planet

You are part of a living planet. Plants play a vital role in keeping Earth alive. Plants form the foundation of the food chain. Living things in all ecosystems depend on them.

Photosynthesis produces and increases plant **biomass**. **Biomass is renewable organic material, which means it is or was living and can be replaced.** It comes from plants, garbage, and animal waste. Wood and fuels are forms of biomass. So are crops such as wheat and corn. Biomass contains stored energy from the Sun.

Plants are vital to a living planet. Plants provide food, energy, and building materials. They do so directly. For example, when you eat a mixed salad of greens, walnuts, and apples, you consume plant food. In fact, you eat biomass. Plants also provide energy indirectly. When a young mother in Darfur lights firewood to cook her family's meal, she accesses biomass. She releases stored energy from the Sun.

Energy in Ecosystems

An ecosystem is a community of organisms that live in an environment. The organisms are interdependent. This means they cannot survive without one another. So they interact and work together.

Sunlight is the powerful energy source for all life on Earth. It sustains both plant and animal life. In an ecosystem, the Sun's energy passes from one organism to another. Plants are the only source of the Sun's energy for animals.

Sun → Producers → Consumers → Decomposers

Producers and Consumers

Through photosynthesis, plants change sunlight energy into chemical energy. Because plants make their own food, they are producers. Producers form the first link of the food chain.

Unlike plants, other organisms can't make food. They must feast on others. Organisms that feed on other organisms are consumers. Consumers form more links in the chain.

Consumers fall into three groups—herbivores, carnivores, and omnivores. You'll learn more about them on the next page.

Did You Know?

Cheetahs are the world's fastest land animals. Shaped for speed, these carnivores dash at 113 kilometers per hour (70 miles per hour). They are fierce hunters who slink through tall grasses to surprise prey.

Success in a hunt means that the cheetah will renew its energy, usually by eating a herbivore.

Zebras are herbivores. They in turn are eaten by carnivores, higher up on the food chain.

Herbivores are vegetarians. They munch only plants. Kangaroos, zebras, and sheep are herbivores.

Scavengers are consumers that eat carrion—rotting, decaying dead animals. Vultures, lobsters, and crows are scavengers. So are bottom-feeding fish such as carp.

Omnivores, including pigs, bears, and opossums, feed on both plants and animals. Are you an omnivore? Many people are.

Energy moves up the chain. At the top, a few mighty predators thrive. **Carnivores are meat-eaters.** Fierce predators such as sharks, tigers, and cheetahs are carnivores. They prey on other animals.

Fungi help remains decay and return nutrients to soil. These decomposers perform an important role in the chain.

Don't Forget the Decomposers!

All the parts of the food chain are linked. One depends on another. What would life be like in an ecosystem that supported only producers and consumers? Over time, plants would snatch all the minerals from soil. Without minerals, these plants would eventually die.

The impact would spread through the chain. What about the herbivores that depend on plants for food? They would have nothing to munch. Lacking plants and herbivores to eat, omnivores would starve, too. Carnivores, at the very top of the chain, would die. This chain reaction would wipe out the ecosystem. That's why the food chain depends on decomposers.

Decomposers do dirty work! They eat the wastes of plants and animals. They also consume plants and animals when they die. Energy from the Sun is stored in those remains.

Fungi, bacteria, and insects are decomposers. They break down nutrients from the dead. Through soil, decomposers launch nutrients back into the ecosystem. How? Plants absorb the nutrients. Stored energy in producers transfers all the way through the chain. Living things live on!

The Madagascar hissing cockroach is a 7.5-centimeter (3-inch) decomposer. Males become miniature battering rams when they battle. They bash each other with their abdomens. Loud hisses warn predators to back off.

The Food Chain

All animals must eat to survive. Many depend on plants for food. The link between plants and animals is a food chain. Some people consider plants the "bottom" of the chain. Actually, plants are the base.

A **hierarchy** is something that shows organization. The food chain is one of nature's most important hierarchies. In this leveling of living things, each feeds on the one below it. As animals do so, energy once stored in plants gets passed along. Which critter eats what? It depends on the habitat and its inhabitants.

Food Chain in a Lake

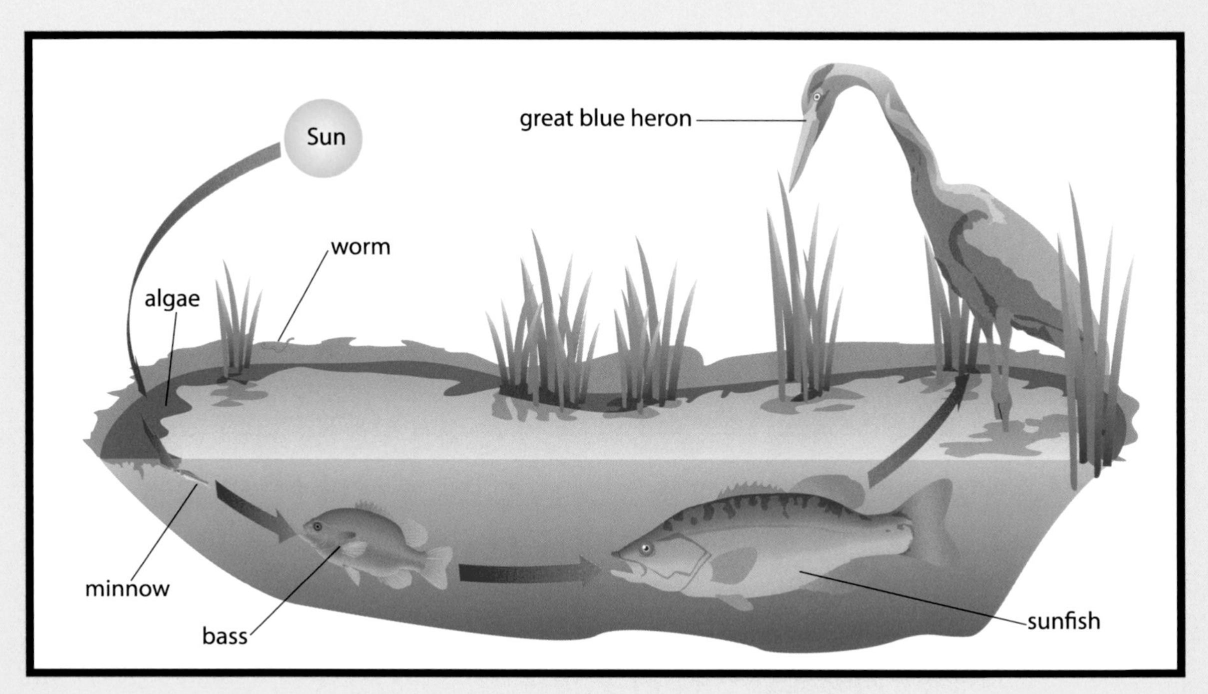

Food Chain in the African Savanna

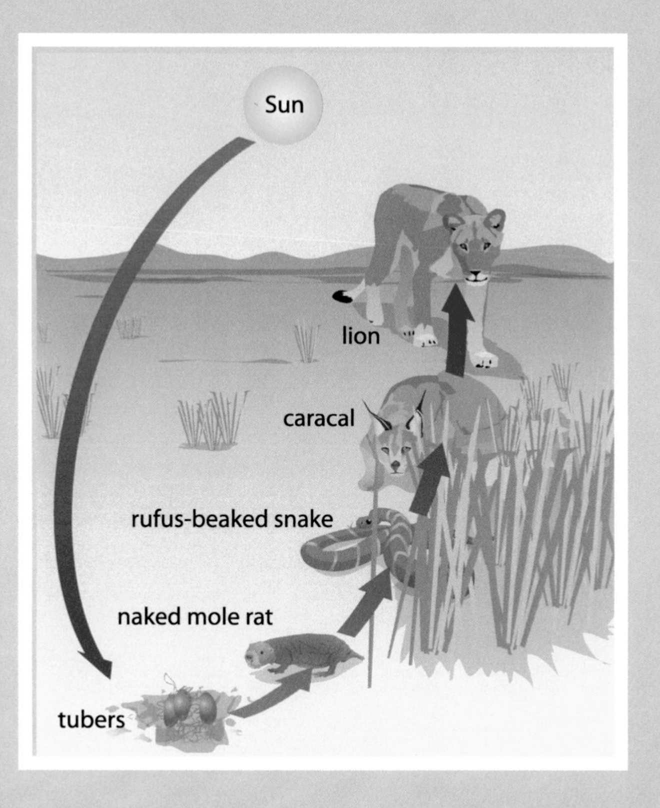

Activity

Choose Your Own Food Chain Adventure!

1. Select one of the habitats.
2. Trace the path of the food chain.
3. Identify which animal eats what.

How does energy from the Sun move through the food chain?
Plants store the Sun's energy. Animals eat plants and other animals and pass the energy along.

What are the three groups of consumers?
They are carnivores, herbivores, and omnivores.

Nutrients from the Soil

You have learned how nutrients travel up from soil and through plants. You have also discovered the important role decomposers play in returning nutrients to soil. Now, let's get our hands dirty as we dig deep into soil, which is Earth's top layer.

Soil is essential for life. Plants, the foundation of the food chain, need soil to thrive. Soil contains all of these: decaying organic materials, living organisms, and nutrients.

Decaying Organic Materials and Living Organisms

What are some decaying materials? Dead plants, including an apple core you might have tossed into a compost heap or dead leaves you raked. How about living organisms? There are weird fungi and microscopic **bacteria**. Plump earthworms and moles burrow through soil. They allow air to move through it.

Moles live in the soil and push nutrients around and create pockets of air as they move.

Nutrients

Plants must have nutrients to grow. Major nutrients found in soil are nitrogen (N), potassium (K), and phosphorus (P). As nutrients become dissolved in water, gnarly roots suck them up.

Depending on where you find it, soil may contain clay, sand, and silt. The best soil has all three. Each impacts soil's texture, or how grainy and sandy it is. In turn, soil's texture influences how well the soil holds onto nutrients and water. Nutrients and water drain away easily from sandy soils, so plants won't grow well. Dense soils of silt and clay are more fertile. Healthy plants grow in abundance, yet water drains poorly.

Nutrients from dense soils of silt provide a great deal of food, as crops, for the people of the world.

Fertilizers

How can farmers increase nutrients in soil and help it hold water? With fertilizer. Fertilizer is made of organic materials, such as manure. (That's animal dung.) Farms mix fertilizer into soil or spread it on top. It's not a plant food. Instead, fertilizer is a nutrient supplier.

Farming requires soil with nutrients.

The "Bloodthirsty" Venus Flytrap

You're traveling through the Green Swamp of North Carolina in the southeastern United States. Decaying plant matter squishes under your feet. Splash! A log rolls in the marshy water—a log with eyes! It's a hungry alligator on the prowl.

You creep through the marsh. You spot it. The endangered plant you've come to observe, a carnivore. Because boggy soil is poor, this beautiful but bloodthirsty plant must find another way to suck up the nutrients it needs to thrive. How? It captures prey, dissolves them, and devours their nutrients.

Does this sound like a creature from a horror film? It's not! It's the Venus flytrap. Here's how this meat-eating plant operates. Its leaves act as jaws. Special cells inside the inner leaf layer are hinges. They hold the jaws open—for now!

The Venus flytrap has found a different way to get its nutrients.

Captured...And Eaten!

Suddenly, an unsuspecting fly settles on the leaves' bristly trigger hairs. In the blink of an eye, hinged leaves snap shut like a trap. The trap squeezes forcefully around its captive. Special glands in the leaves digest the captive insect. It's a process that lasts from five to twelve days. During that time, the plant liquefies the gooey inner parts of the fly. Unable to digest the protective exoskeleton (hard outer shell), the plant holds it in its trap like a turkey carcass after a holiday meal. In time, wind howls over the bog. The exoskeleton blows away.

Did You Know?

If a nonedible item such as a stone or twig falls into the flytrap's mouth, then the plant will spit it out. Yuck!

What are the three major plant nutrients?
They are nitrogen (N), potassium (K), and phosphorus (P).

What is soil, and what is it made of?
It's the top layer of Earth. It's made of decaying organic materials, living organisms, and nutrients.

How does the Venus flytrap obtain nutrients in an environment with poor soil?
It captures insects and dissolves them.

Early Investigations, Early Discoveries

Jan Baptista van Helmont and Joseph Priestley's investigations paved the way in learning about photosynthesis.

Who Are You?

It's sometime before 1639 near Brussels, Belgium. You wonder how plants obtain food that makes them grow. You theorize soil feeds them and set out to prove it. You fill an earthen pot with 200 pounds of dried soil and plant a five-pound willow shoot in it. You record these weights accurately. Over the next five years, you carefully water the shoot.

Finally, you remove it from the pot and weigh it. A shoot no longer, the willow weighs in at a whopping 169 pounds! You dry and weigh the soil. It's only lost about 2 ounces. You come to the conclusion that the plant hasn't taken nutrients from the soil. If it had, then the soil would have lost weight.

"Thus, 164 pounds of wood, bark, and roots had arisen from water alone," you declare.

Jan Baptista van Helmont

Well… no. Yet, your famous "willow experiment" is a milestone. Your scientific measurements and notes are exact. You've completed one of the first recorded examples of the scientific method. Who are you?
Jan Baptista van Helmont, a Flemish chemist.

Germinate Seeds

Do plants need soil to grow? Germinate seeds to find out! You will need seeds, a paper towel, water, and a plastic bag.

- Use quick-sprouting seeds, such as lima beans or radishes.
- Soak the paper towel with water. Then spread the seeds on the towel. Fold the towel in two. Place it inside the plastic bag.
- Now, locate a safe area to store the bag. It shouldn't be too sunny or drafty.
- Check on your seeds in three days. What's happened? Create a before-and-after illustration of the seeds. (Hang onto those germinated seeds. Keep them moist. You'll need them for a later activity on page 39.)

Who Are You?

It's 1772. Like your friend Ben Franklin, you're fascinated by science. Although you've never formally studied it, you love to tinker. Today, you're performing an experiment in Leeds, England. Earlier, you placed a sprig of mint and a burning candle into a jar. You sealed it. In time, the flame died.

Now, after 10 days, you attempt to light the candle again. With a mirror, you direct sunlight over the wick. The flame flickers feebly once, twice, three times. Suddenly, the candle brightly burns.

You don't know it. Yet, thanks to a simple sprig of mint, there's oxygen to fuel the flame. You also don't realize it. Yet, you're the first person to observe photosynthesis, the plant's release of oxygen. Pretty impressive! Who are you? **Joseph Priestley, a chemist and minister**.

Van Helmont and Priestley's investigations were important stepping-stones. Yet, these curious chemists weren't aware of photosynthesis.

Joseph Priestley

Jan Baptista van Helmont

Who?	Jan Baptista van Helmont, 1579?–1644
What?	Determined plants don't get food from soil
When?	Before 1639?
Where?	Brussels, Belgium
How?	Conducted "willow experiment"

Joseph Priestley

Who?	Joseph Priestley, 1733–1804
What?	First observed photosynthesis
When?	1772
Where?	Leeds, England
How?	Lit a candle in a sealed jar with water and mint

Did You Know?

Joseph Priestley discovered oxygen, which he called "fire air." He created "laughing gas," nitrous oxide. Dentists and doctors would later use this gas as an anesthetic, which prevents a patient from feeling pain.

HEY, WHAT HAPPENS...

Aquatic (water) plants, including algae, have no leaves. They conduct photosynthesis by taking in water directly. They obtain CO_2 from water. During wintertime, photosynthesis stops. Plants and trees live off stored food supplies.

...If Plants Have No Leaves?

A leaf's main job is to make food. So, what happens if a plant has no leaves?

Water plants such as algae and seaweed aren't true plants. They don't have roots, stems, or leaves. That means they lack a transportation system. Yet, they still perform photosynthesis. How? Unlike land plants, seaweed and algae take in nutrients directly from water. They obtain carbon dioxide from water, rather than air.

You can see the red algae in this pond.

Seaweed snatches sunlight with **chlorophyll**. That's the same green pigment in land plants. Has deep-red or rich-brown algae ever tickled your ankles in a lake or pond? Those algae contain different-colored pigments. Blue, red, gold, or brown, they catch rays the way chlorophyll does.

This is a closeup photo of water bubbles surrounding algae.

Activity

Oxygen Bubbles

Observe oxygen bubbles produced by aquatic plants. You'll need a glass jar and a water plant, such as elodea. (You can usually find this in a pet shop.) You'll also need an aquarium filled with water and placed in a sunny area.

- First, totally sink the jar in the aquarium. Be certain that there's no air inside the jar.
- Next, place the jar directly over the plant. Check to be sure the jar is totally filled with water.
- Over a one-hour period, check for changes every 20 minutes.
- Draw what you see after an hour. What evidence can you find that proves photosynthesis has occurred? Bubbles indicate oxygen is present.

...During Winter?

During shorter, colder, dryer days of winter, outside of the tropics, photosynthesis can't take place. Without water and sunlight, plants can't work their wonders. So how do plants react? Starting in fall, food factories close for the season.

The leaves of these trees have changed into spectacular colors.

Deciduous trees are fall transformers. Do you live in an area where tree leaves change color in the fall? Then you've observed food factories close. First, cells in stems begin to die. There's no longer a transportation system available. **Nutrients and water can't travel through trees. As a result, chlorophyll in leaves breaks down.** Leaves lose their green color. Different pigments become noticeable. Leaves change in elaborate bursts of color. Spectacular shades of maroon, orange, and gold take over.

When cells in stems die off, leaves fall away from branches. They flutter to the ground.

During winter, trees and plants become dormant (they stop growing and seem to rest). Fortunately, they spent all summer turning extra food into **starch** and stashing it. Because of that survival plan, trees and plants live off stored food supplies. When winter melts into spring, food factories crank back into production.

Did You Know?

Evergreens stay gloriously green throughout winter. Why? They perform photosynthesis year round. Their bristly needles are actually leaves! Firmly rolled and covered with a waxy shield, needles conserve water.

With their ability to conserve water, evergreens withstand harsh winters.

<u>How do aquatic plants take in carbon dioxide?</u>
They obtain it from water.

<u>How do they capture sunlight?</u>
With chlorophyll and other pigments.

<u>How do trees stay alive during winter?</u>
They live off stored starch.

<u>Make a list of changes that take place in plants and trees during fall and winter.</u>

Respiration

Respiration does the opposite of photosynthesis. Performed day and night, respiration allows plants to obtain energy from food.

Once plants have snatched solar energy, what do they do with it? Plants tap into **carbohydrates**, such as **starch**, created and stored in photosynthesis. They use oxygen to break down, or "burn," sugar and get energy from food. As a result, plants give off water and carbon dioxide. This process is called respiration.

You've learned respiration is a life process. People and animals must respire to live. Plants also respire. They need stored chemical energy to carry out life processes.

Respiration occurs in plant **cells**. Through respiration, plants release carbon dioxide and take in oxygen from the air. That's the reverse of photosynthesis, in which oxygen is released and carbon dioxide is taken in.

Equation for Respiration

Plants convert carbohydrates to energy. The equation for respiration uses symbols for the process.

$$C_6H_{12}O_6 + 6O_2 \rightarrow 6CO_2 + 6H_2O + (\text{energy})$$

glucose + oxygen → carbon dixode + water + (energy)

How does the equation translate? **Glucose and oxygen break down to release carbon dioxide, water, and energy.**

You've learned **chloroplasts** are the **organelles** that work magic in photosynthesis. In respiration, other organelles take over. Mitochondria are cell powerhouses. These oblong organelles convert food to energy.

Plants use released energy to stay alive. With it, they grow and reproduce. But it doesn't end with plants. Respiration is a **chemical reaction**. How does the reaction get passed to animals and people? Yep, through the ever-reliable food chain!

Did You Know?

Every part of a plant respires—from roots, to stems, to leaves, to flowers.

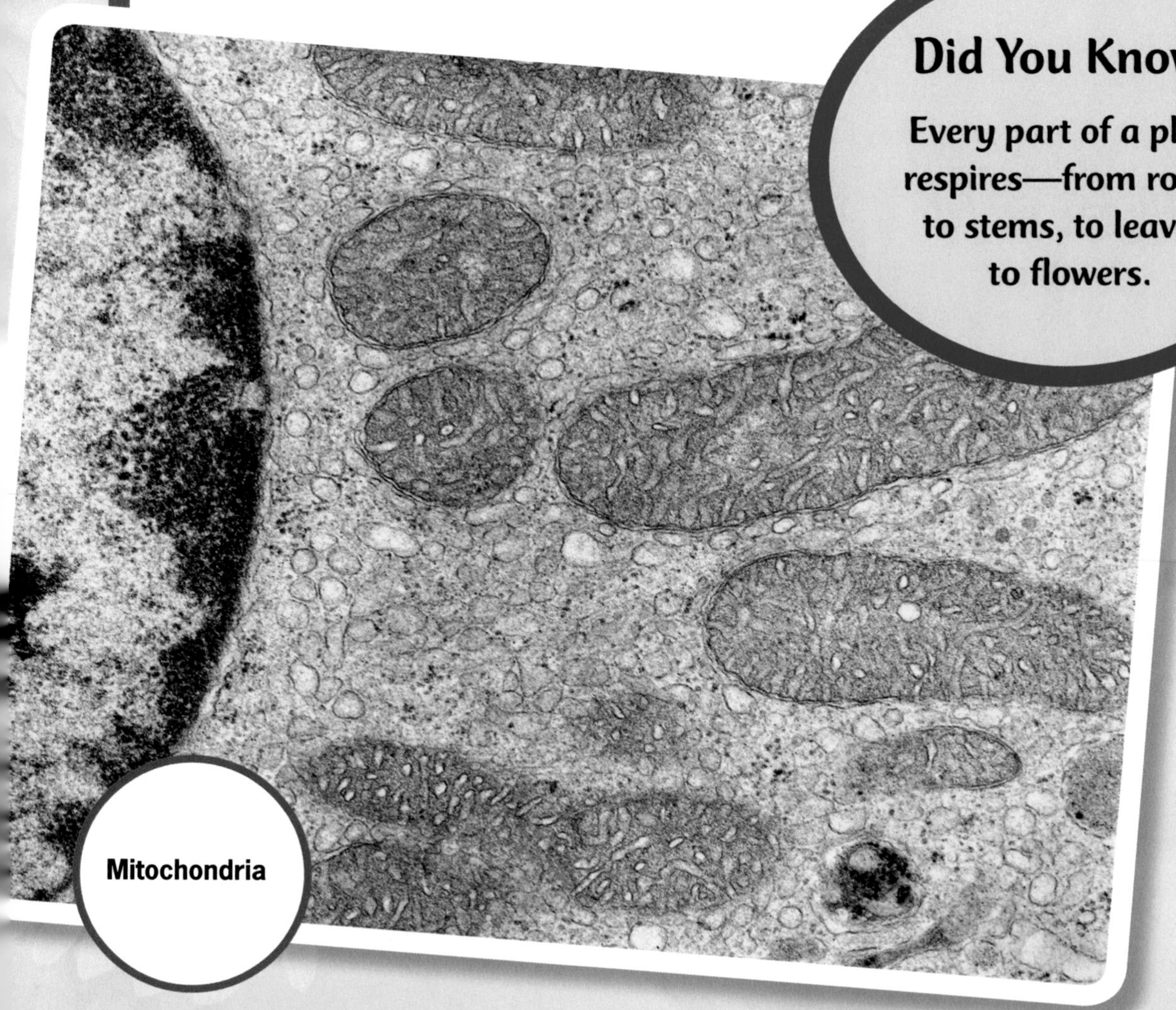

Mitochondria

The Opposite of Photosynthesis

Respiration and photosynthesis work together. Many people say respiration "does the opposite of photosynthesis." This means the activities of photosynthesis and respiration are opposites.

For example, since photosynthesis needs sunlight, it takes place *only* during daytime. That's when plants take in carbon dioxide and release oxygen. However, respiration takes place day *and* night. Then, plants do the reverse of photosynthesis. They take in oxygen, and they release carbon dioxide.

Photosynthesis stores energy. It builds up carbohydrates and makes food. Respiration does the opposite. It releases energy. It breaks down carbohydrates and uses food.

You've learned photosynthesis shuts down in winter months. During that time, respiration slows, too. In the warmth of spring, when plants bud and leaves grow, photosynthesis starts again. And then, respiration increases.

Tropical plants like this that live at or near the equator provide a lot of the planet's oxygen through photosynthesis.

Activity

Energy in Respiration

Do you still have those germinating seeds from page 29? You will need them for this activity. You'll also need a test tube, a cotton ball, and a thermometer.

- First, place the seeds into the tube.
- Then, place the thermometer inside the tube so that it touches the seeds.
- Now, plug the base of the tube with the cotton ball.
- Observe any change in temperature. Released energy should cause it to rise.

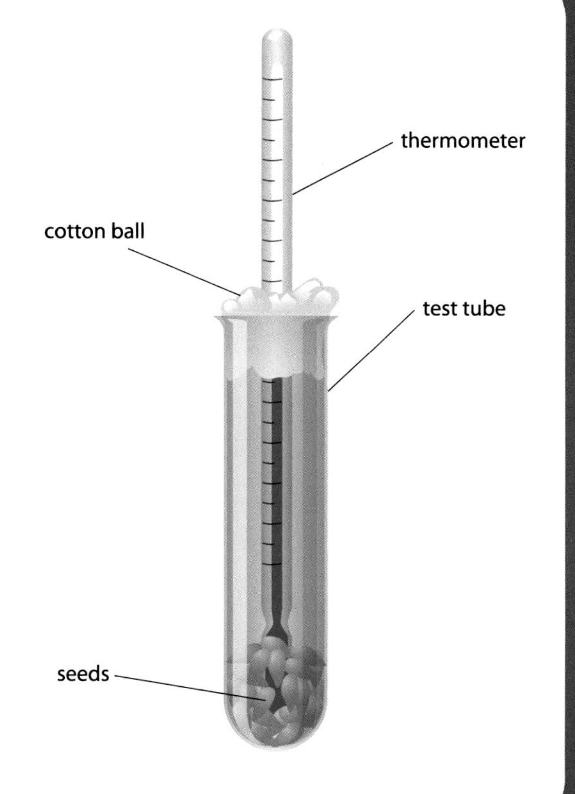

Did You Know?

The more a plant weighs, the more it respires.

What process do plants use to convert carbohydrates to energy?
Respiration.

Photosynthesis takes place only during the day. When does respiration take place?
Both day and night.

Which parts of plant cells convert food to energy?
Mitochondria.

Destroying the Lungs of the World

The world's lush rainforests are nicknamed "the Lungs of the World." Why? Magnificent rainforest trees clean air. Through photosynthesis, trees take in carbon dioxide. They release oxygen. Scientists estimate rainforests supply nearly 40% of Earth's oxygen—oxygen living things require for survival.

Chainsaws, Axes, and Flames

People are destroying the precious Lungs of the World at an alarming rate. Deforestation is the culprit. **Deforestation is the removal of rainforests through burning, cutting, and clearing.** People wield chainsaws and axes. They chop down ancient trees in quests for oil and gas. To clear land for farming, ranching, and industry, people ignite raging fires. These fires pour carbon dioxide into the air. This creates greenhouse gases that raise Earth's temperature and contribute to global warming.

The removal of rainforests is having a negative impact on the planet and its food chains.

What Can You Do?

It might be easy to think rainforests are far removed from your life. Yet, you're a vital link in a global chain. How can you conserve wood and wood products to reduce the number of trees destroyed?

- Encourage your family and friends to purchase paper products made from recycled paper. Notepads, pocket folders, napkins, tissues, toilet paper—all can be produced in environmentally friendly fashions.
- Ask adults to purchase certified wood products. If a product is certified, then trees used to make it were legally chopped down. Organizations such as the Sustainable Forestry Initiative in North America are on the lookout for illegal logging.
- Promise to one day plant a tree. By planting trees, you reduce greenhouse gases. Breathing buddies take in carbon dioxide. They release oxygen. No wonder scientists believe photosynthesis is the most important process on Earth!

This label helps you know that the furniture was made using certified wood.

Rainforest ecosystems are alive with animal and plant life. The vibrantly colored red-eyed tree frog of South and Central America is not yet considered threatened in its natural environment.

Activity

Think one person can't make a difference? Think again!

Develop Do and Don't lists. Then, launch them into action.

Wild and wonderful plants

The carnivorous pitcher plant

The pitcher plant is a meat-eating bog-dweller. Its leaves are shaped like water jugs. Like pitchers, they fill with rainwater. On the rim of each pitcher, sweet nectar lures insects with a yummy scent. An unsuspecting ant wanders over the rim. It slips on the slick surface. Inside the leaf, stubbly, downward-pointing hairs snatch the hapless insect. Down, down, down it slides to pooled rainwater, where it drowns. Special glands in the leaves digest the captive for its nutrients. Yuck!

World's tallest living thing

The gigantic General Sherman tree looms in California's Sequoia National Park. At 275 feet (84 metres) tall, the sequoia stretches taller than the Statue of Liberty and London's Tower Bridge! Named after the American Civil War general, William T. Sherman, the tree is over 2,100 years old.

jungle

The Titan Arum may look pretty, but it can smell like rotting meat!

WORLD'S STINKIEST PLANT

Pheew, this plant reeks! The Titan Arum blooms wild only in the Indonesian rainforests of Sumatra. This stinker is known as "the corpse flower". It sprouts from tubers that weigh as much as a person – 77 kilograms (170 pounds). Why does it smell so rancid? To attract decomposers such as carrion beetles!

Respiration and Photosynthesis Quiz

You've learned about photosynthesis. You know it's the process plants use to make their own food using water, air, and sunlight. Now, take this quiz to check up on what you've learned!

Fill in the Blank

1. Plants take in ___________.
2. Plants release ________.
3. Three major plant organs are __________, __________, and __________.
4. __________ in plants trap sunlight for photosynthesis.
5. ___________ is the pigment that gives plants their bright green color.

Multiple Choice

1. _____ eat both plants and animals.

   a. Carnivores

   b. Omnivores

   c. Herbivores

   d. Algae

2. Solar energy is energy_____.

   a. from the Sun

   b. from respiration

   c. from photosynthesis

   d. from the food chain

3. Photosynthesis takes place during the day, while respiration takes place_____.

   a. in dead plants

   b. in the afternoon

   c. at night

   d. day and night

4. What are the organelles in which respiration takes place?

   a. mitochondria

   b. epidermis

   c. chloroplasts

   d. stomata

5. One carbohydrate plants produce in photosynthesis is _____.

a. starch

b. stomata

c. oxygen

d. pigment

Short Answer

1. What is translocation?

2. Explain how the Sun's energy is passed to humans through the food chain.

Illustrations

1. Make a drawing that shows how photosynthesis works. Drawings will vary.

2. Make a drawing to illustrate how respiration works. Drawings will vary.

Answer Key

1. Carbon dioxide
2. Oxygen
3. Leaves, stems, and roots
4. Chloroplasts
5. Chlorophyll

1. b
2. a
3. d
4. a
5. a

1. Possible response: Translocation is the movement of minerals and water within a plant.
2. Possible response: Plants capture the Sun's energy and use it to make their own food in a chemical reaction. Herbivores eat the plants. Then omnivores or carnivores eat the herbivores. By eating plants and/or animals, people receive the Sun's energy.

Glossary

Algae A marine plant with no leaves, roots, or stems; includes seaweed and kelp

Bacteria Single-celled microorganisms

Biomass Renewable, organic material that comes from plants, garbage, and animal waste

Carbohydrate Produced by plants in photosynthesis and a source of energy for animals and people; sugar and starch are carbohydrates

Cell Basic, microscopic part of a living thing

Chemical reaction Reaction that occurs when two chemicals react together to form new chemicals

Chlorophyll Green pigment in plants that gives them their color

Chloroplast Organelle of a plant in which photosynthesis takes place

Cuticle Waxy protective covering of a plant's epidermis

Dermal tissue Plant tissue that protects soft plant parts

Epidermis Outside layer of cells on a plant

Ground tissue Plant tissue that supports stems and roots

Hierarchy Way of organizing something or breaking it into levels

Mesophyll Short tissues, found between layers of leaves, that contain chloroplasts

Organelle Little part, among many, that makes up a cell and has its own function

Palisade parenchyma Layer of long cells beneath a plant's epidermis; contains chloroplasts

Phloem Plant tissue that moves sugar manufactured in photosynthesis throughout a plant

Photosynthesis Process by which green plants use energy from the Sun to make food

Respiration Process by which cells obtain energy through combining food and oxygen

Solar energy Energy from the Sun

Spongy mesophyll Leaf tissue that contains chloroplasts

Starch Carbohydrate made by plants

Stomata Tiny pores in the outer layers of plants that take in air and allow water to pass

Translocation Movement of minerals and fluids through a plant

Vascular tissue Plant tissue that transports materials throughout the plant

Xylem Plant tissue that carries minerals and water from plant roots

Further Information

Books to read

Blackaby, Susan. ***Green and Growing: A Book About Plants***. Mankato, MN: Picture Window Books, 2005.

Cherry, Lynne, and Gary Braasch. ***How We Know What We Know About Our Changing Climate: Scientists and Kids Explore Global Warming***. Nevada City, CA: Dawn Publications, 2008.

Hopkins, William G. ***Photosynthesis and Respiration***. Langhorne, PA: Chelsea House, 2006.

Jakab, Cheryl. ***The Plant Life Cycle***. Bel Air, CA: Smart Apple Media, 2007.

Silverstein, Alvin, Virginia B. Silverstein, and Laura Silverstein Nunn. ***Science Concepts: Photosynthesis***. Minneapolis, MN: Twenty-First Century Books, 2007.

Stille, Darlene R. ***Plant Cells: The Building Blocks of Plants***. Mankato, MN: Compass Point Books, 2006.

Tocci, Salvatore. ***Experiments with Plants***. Danbury, CT: Children's Press, 2002.

Websites

FactHound Offers a safe, fun way to find Internet sites related to this book. All of the sites on FactHound have been researched by our staff.

Visit *www.facthound.com*

Index